Angel-A

For AngelA

"The stars the angels the heavens the…

Dreams the…

Angels here…they

Help us get to

Heaven." RL Lane

Introduction: On and on we marched that day. Talking and marching and marching and talking…

The day comes just once a year. A day to remember. Memorial Day 2015.

The day comes just once in a lifetime. A day to remember him. Memorial Day 2015.

I knew she needed a whole book. The drawing and the person. I guess they both really needed a whole book. He did because it was his favorite drawing. My Uncle Eddy. She did because she is the angel. AngelA. I drew the angel drawing after she came back into my life.

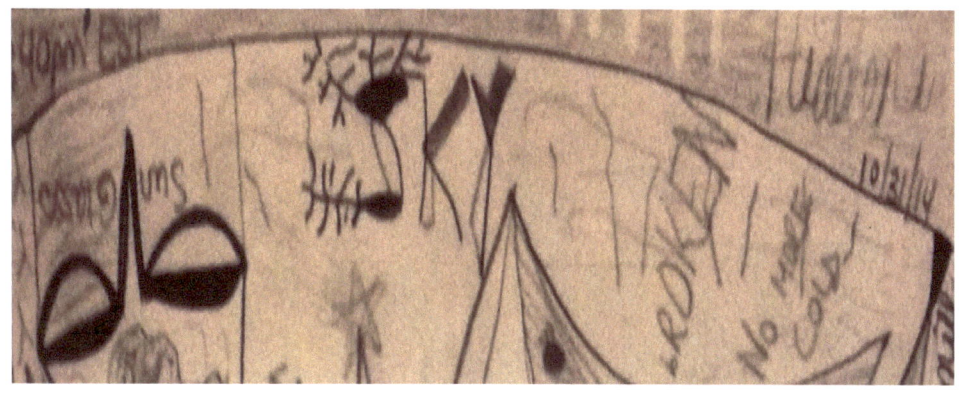

Thy "S" of "SKY" has reindeer antlers

And I see a fish shape too

Written on the façade of a rock

"Sunglasses" is written upside-down

I turned the picture around to see the

Eyes and pointed nose

Is she a witch?

One eye is clear

The other is not

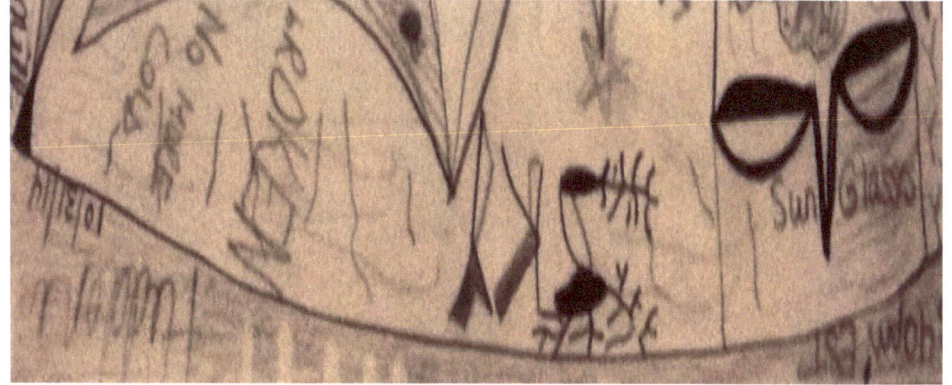

She is not a witch. She is like no other person I know. *Well, we could say that about a lot of people, but it is true about her.*

He was like no other person I knew. Anyone who knew him would agree.

People are intimidated by her beauty. Surely she must not be smart. Why would God give just one person both? *Well he did...*

He would listen to my stories and then he would read me his. He would usually cry by the time he got to the end. That is how much his words meant to him. He sure did like his words. He knew a lot of them.

The flags were all there that Memorial Day. Army, Navy, Marine Corps, Air Force. We looked at each of them. All honorable. Each different but all standing for the same valour. Which one is better? *Why would you compare them?*

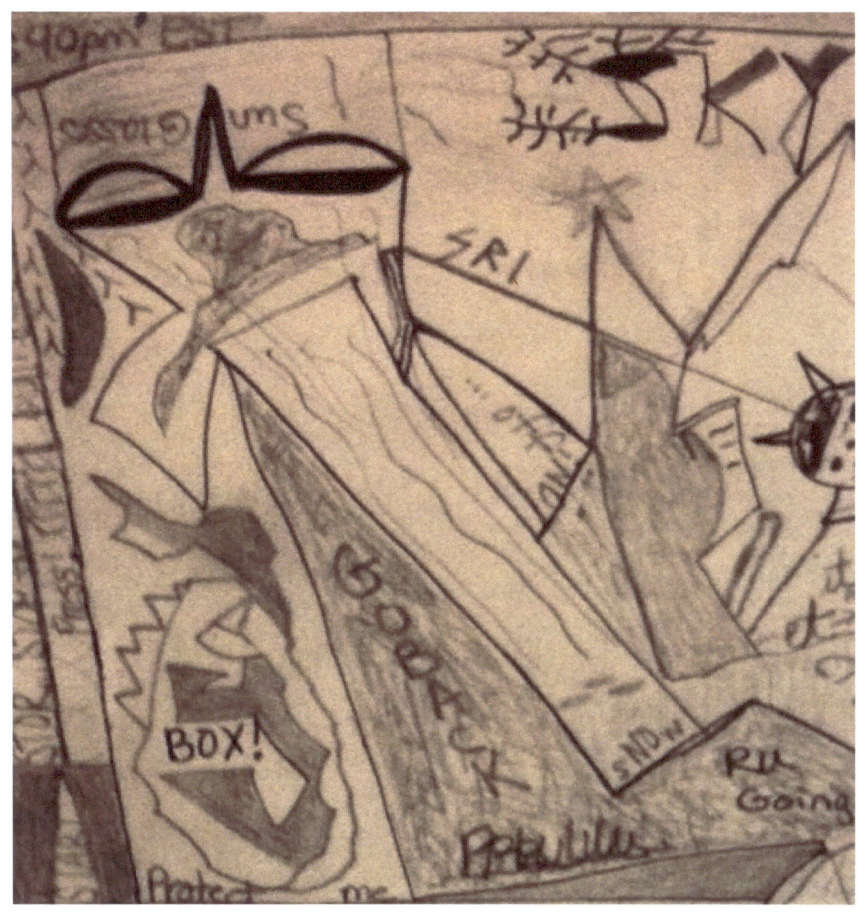

I see a blog…log

Two spirits together

One with a book

I don't think it is the bible

I see the other spirit

With his boxing gloves

Then there is another one

A spirit holding a newspaper

Just like my Dad that night I saw him

50 days after his death

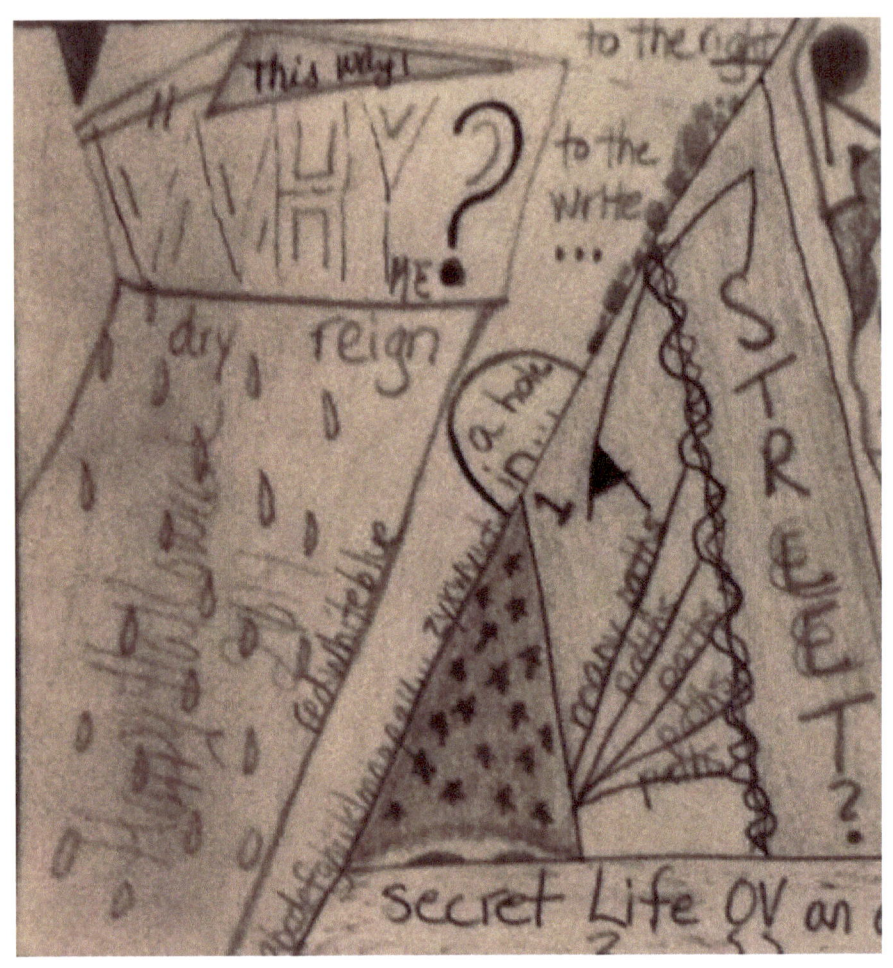

WHY?

"This way", I had written
A wizard just peaking above

secret Life OV an antE

Many paths leading to the STREET?

A fishing pole and a hook catching the "S"

It was Halloween I recorded the date

Dry reign with raindrops red white and blue

Would the red white and blue ever reign again?

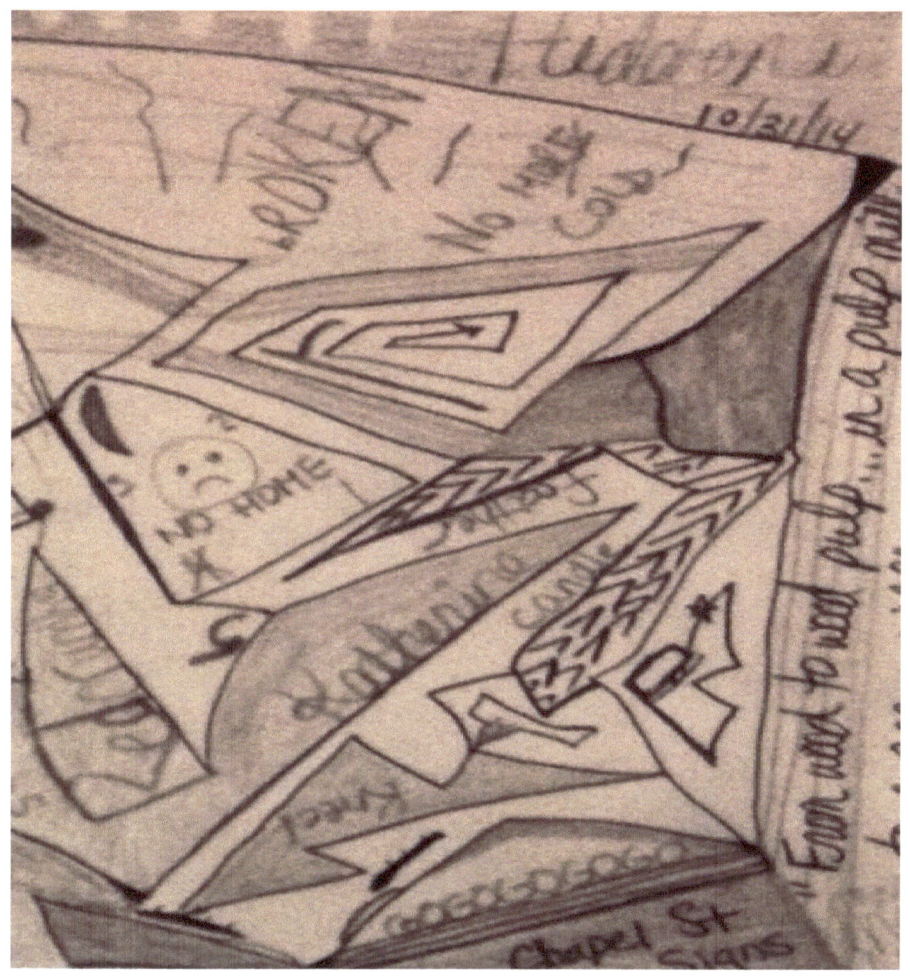

"Chapel Street Signs" is in the bottom

I had it all done

But then the drawings appeared starting with this angel

And RL Lane's books were changed forever

Her old hobo man

It is true he had no home

He could have had a home

But instead he rode the rails

One of my favorite sayings…

"From wood to wood pulp in a pulp mill to a paper mill…

Then we write…"

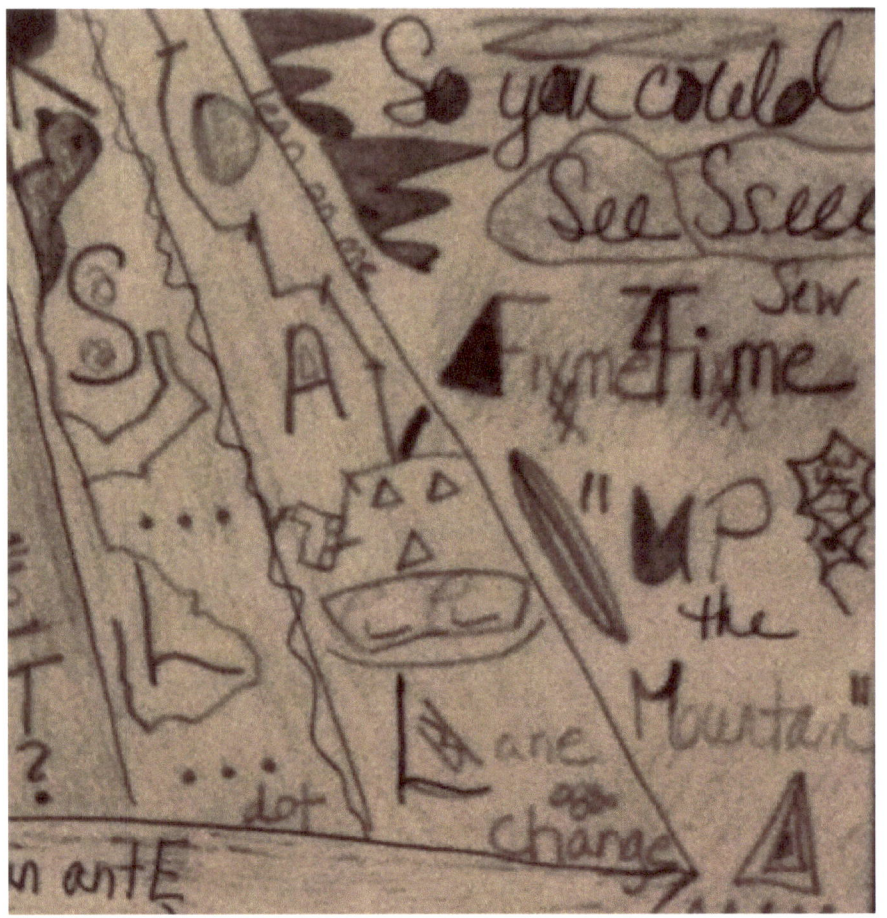

Well, it was Halloweed…Halloween when I drew her

So I guess that is why there is a pumpkin face

Apparently I still needed to be fixed

The arrow was already pointing up the mountain

Could I be sewn back together

Once I got to the other side?

Would I grow like their flowers and vegetables?

Or would I just be a weed?

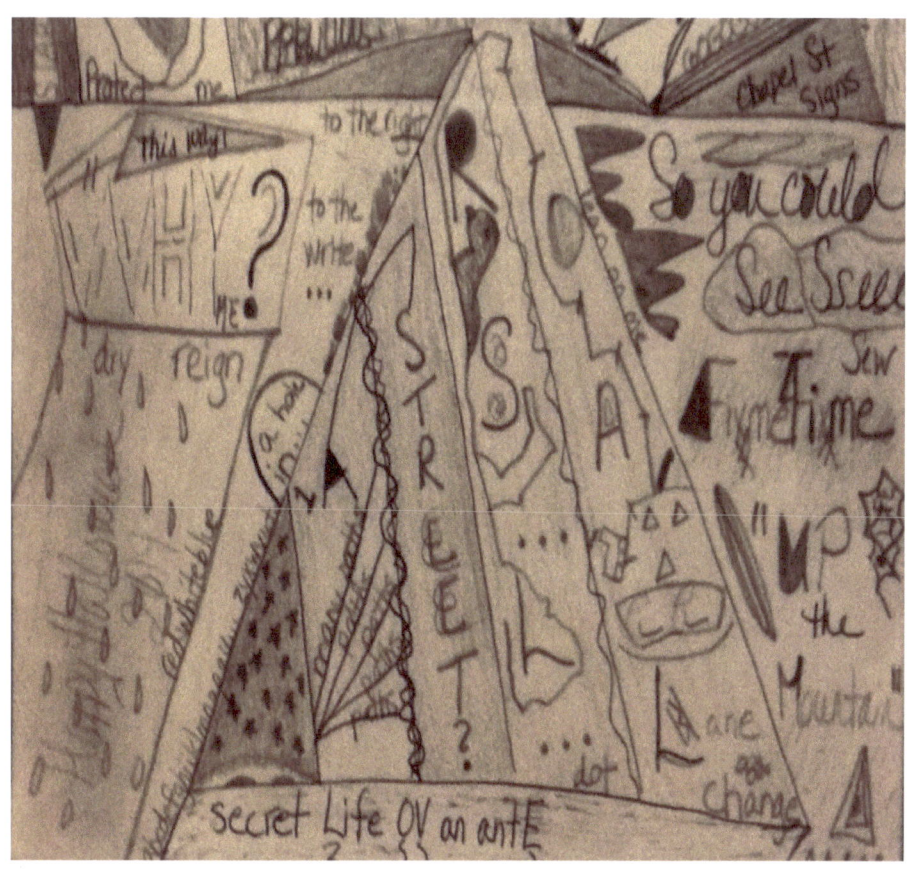

I'll put her back together for you.

Here is the bottom of the dress.

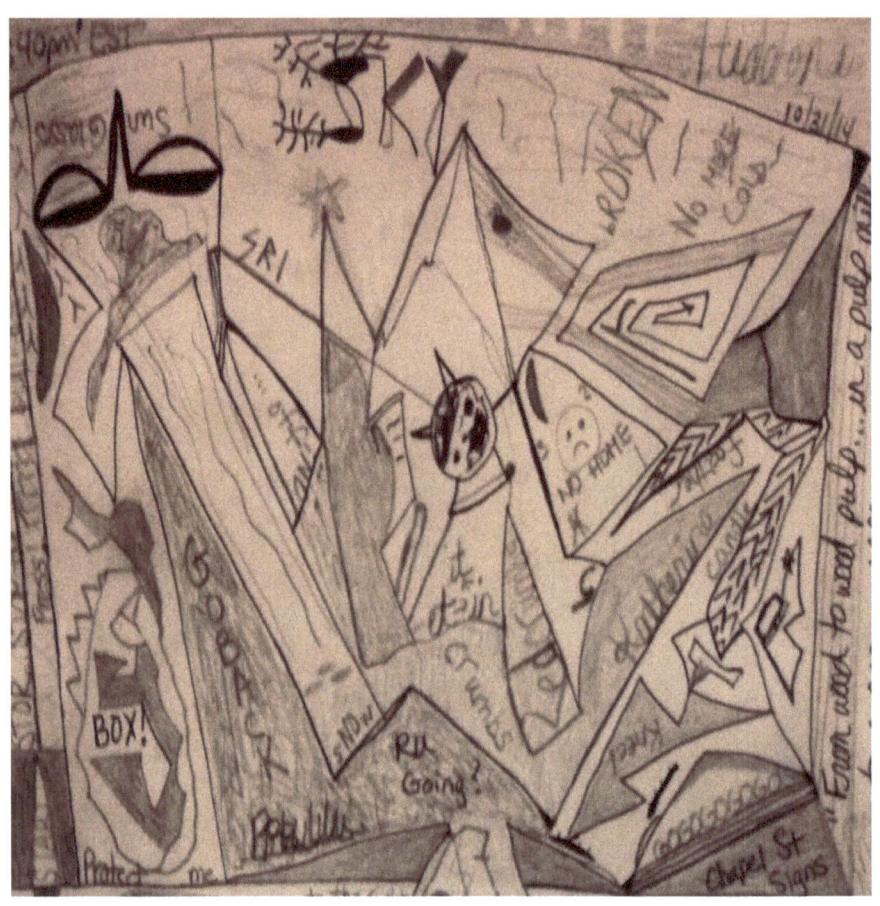

Here is the top of her.

I still don't know why that cat is there

The one that looks like a robot

Or a cat from Mars

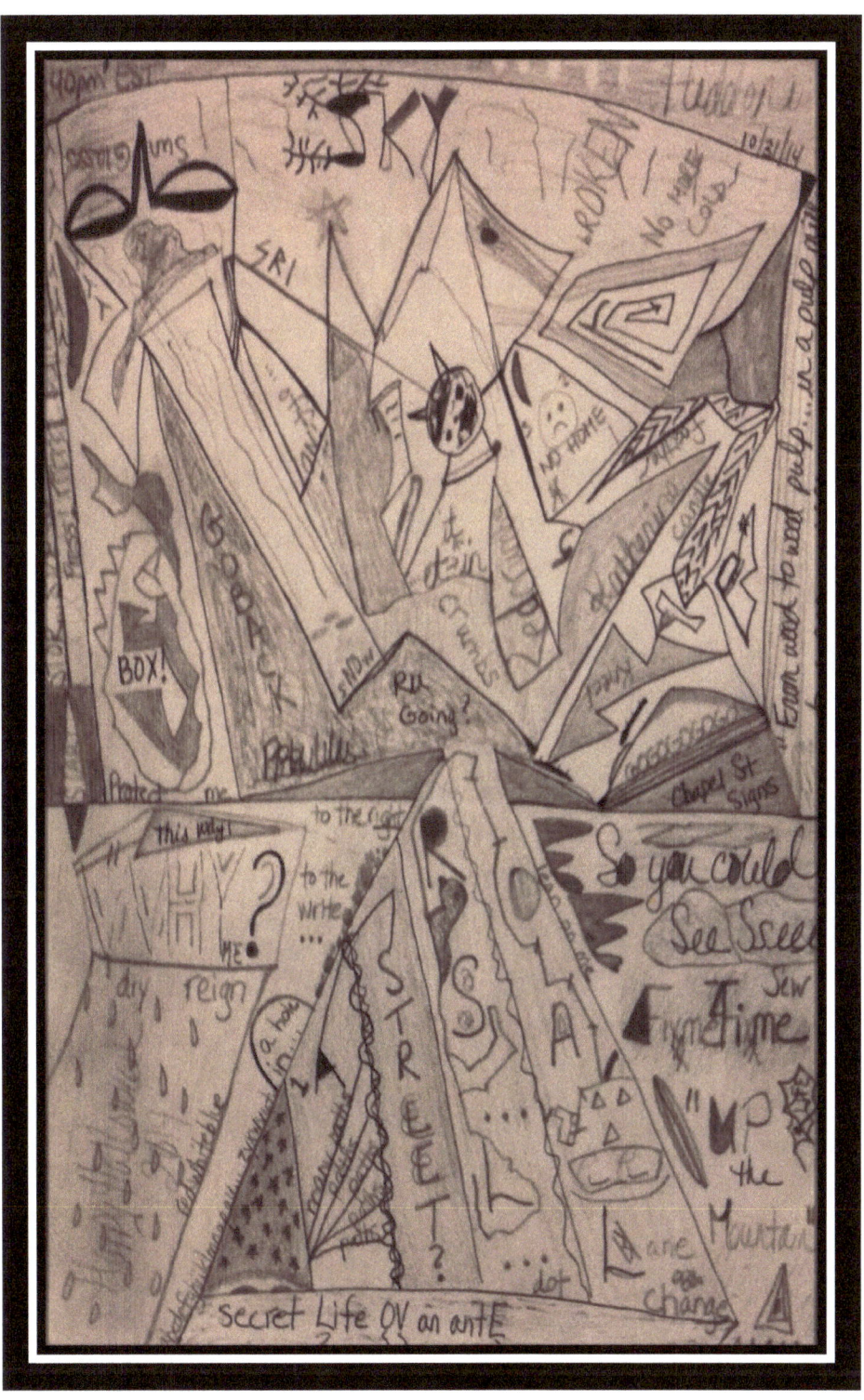

Here she is together again.

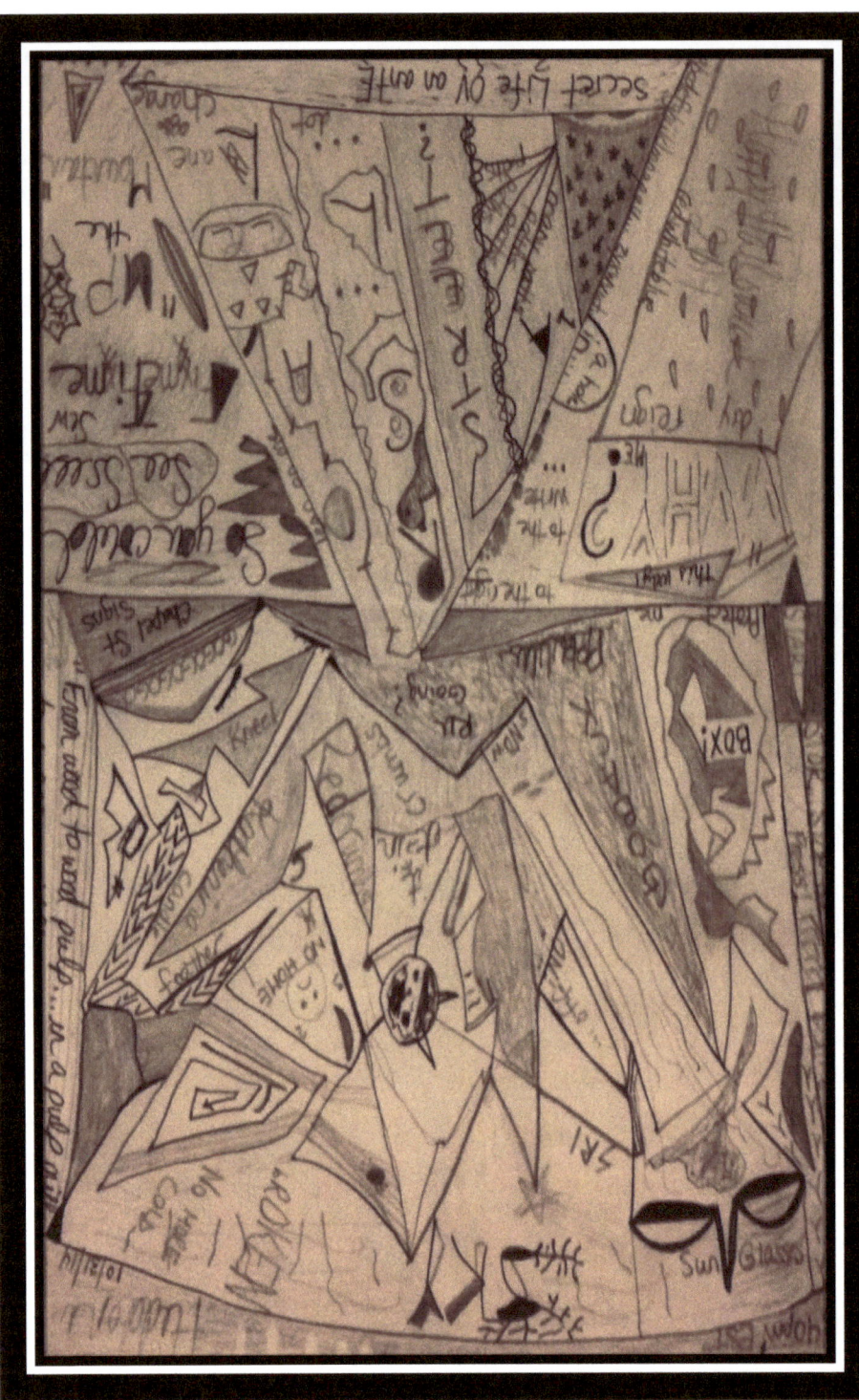

Here she is upside-down.

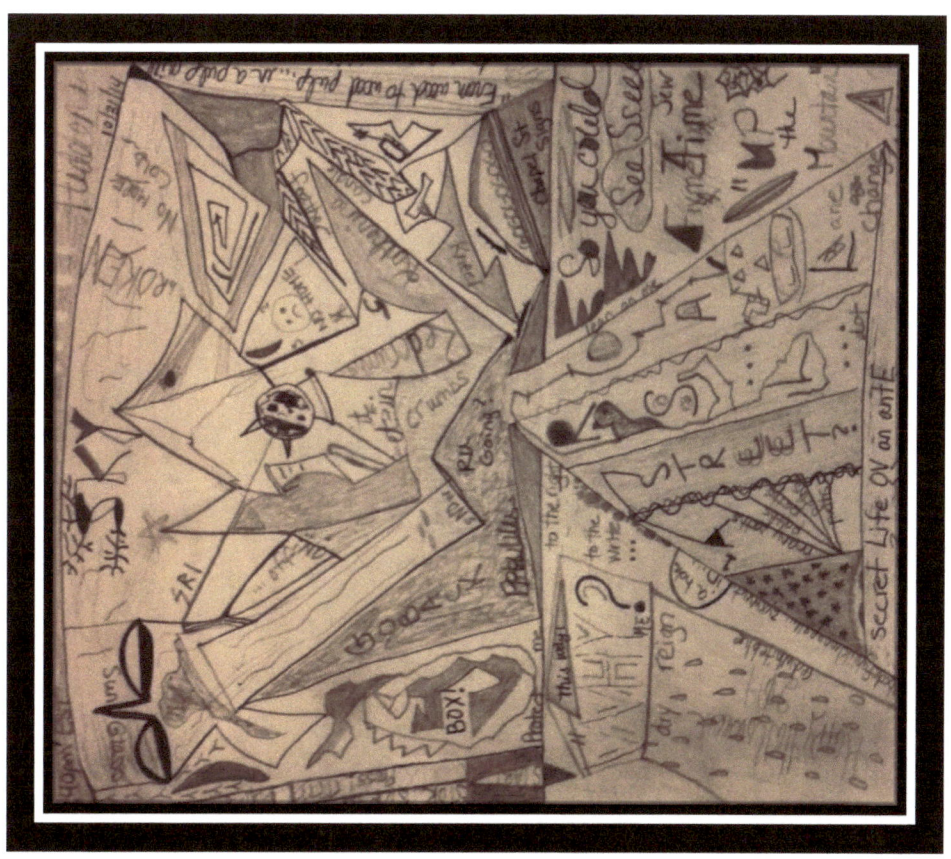

Here she is sideways. I had no idea what I was drawing when I was creating her. I feel like I am missing something about her…there is something about her I am not seeing…

Let me know

If you figure it out

It is my drawing

So I should know

What it is about

She is beautifule to me. AngelA.

He was beautifule to me. Uncle Eddy.

He loved poems

He did not like mine

He could write poems

I read one of his

beautifule it was

He used a lot of big words

My words are so simple

But my heart is the same

What I want to do is the same

I want people to read these words

And to feel something

Anything

I want people to think

Something

Anything

Whatever they want however they want

I needed this to be at least 20 pages long. This art book. So I am adding this page here. What can I tell you? What would you like to know? Do you know RL Lane? Oddly enough, people think they do, but I can assure you they do not. I do love the name. RL Lane. People have asked me how long I will use the name. I actually am not sure yet. She was the name for the beginning of the EcarreT series, so I may never want her to go...

Oh. I actually needed at least 24 pages.

I have hundreds of drawings at this point, and I honestly still never have any idea what I am drawing. Here are a few of the latest…

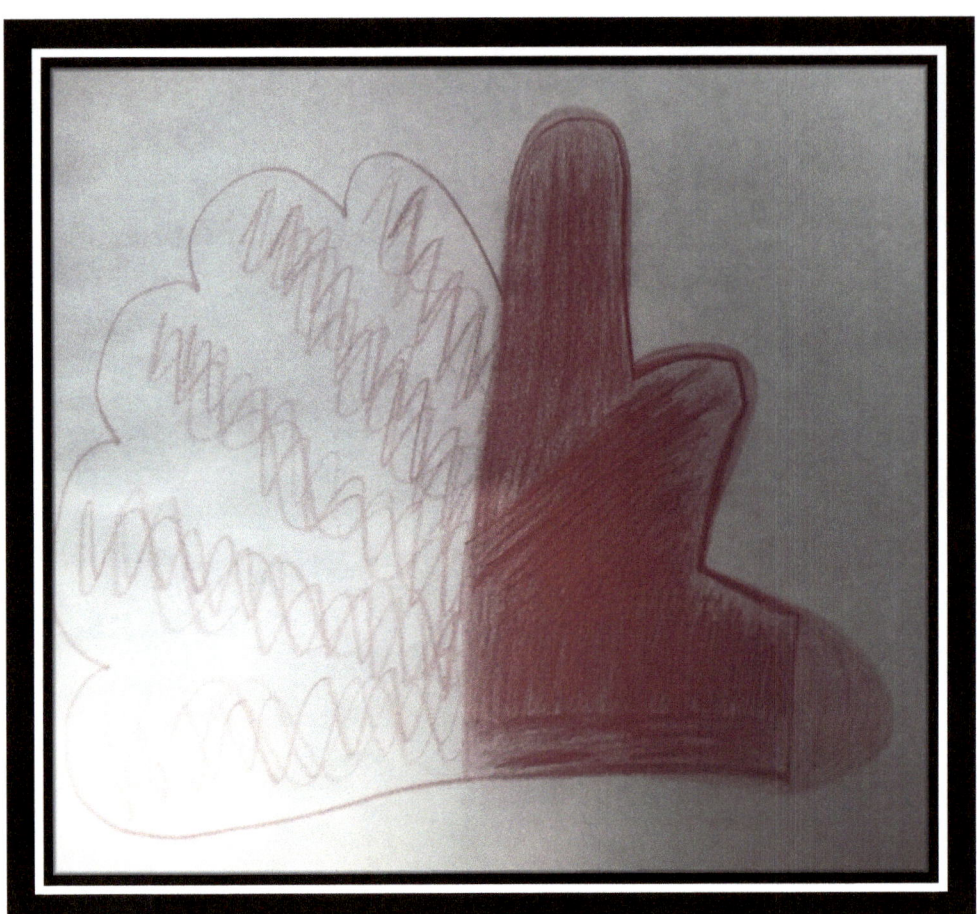

The eagle flying above

Giving her a hand

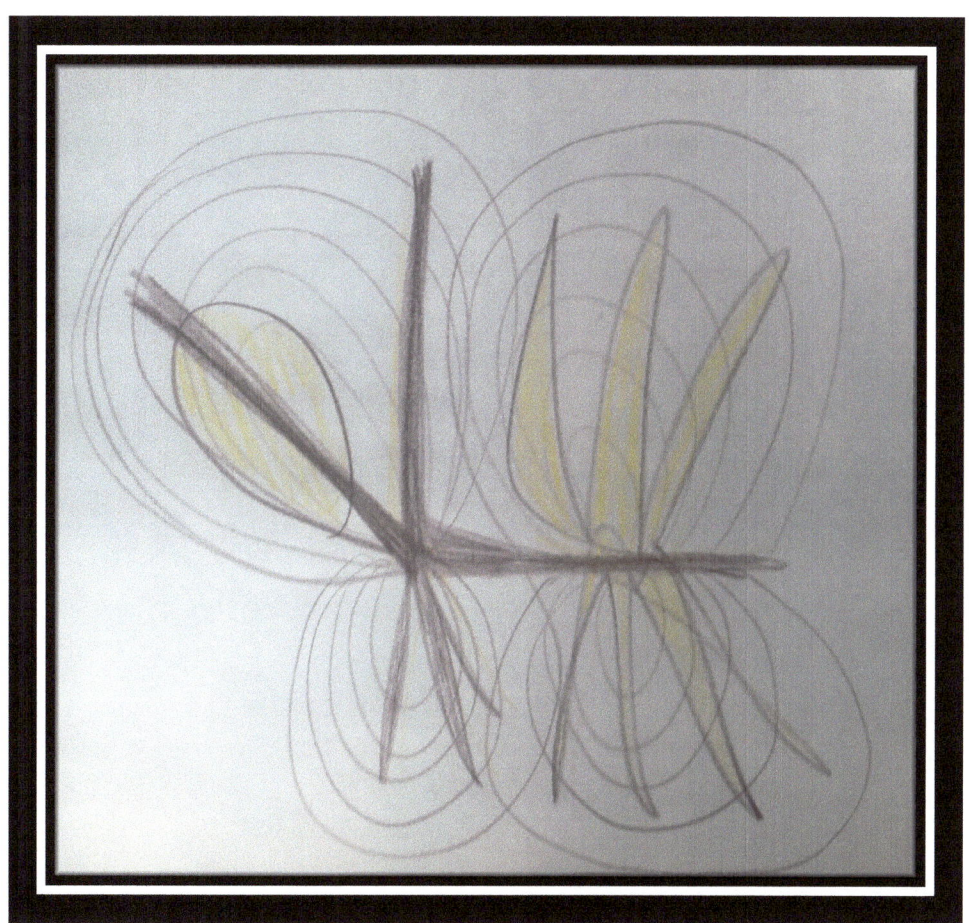

Remember your roots

They keep on saying

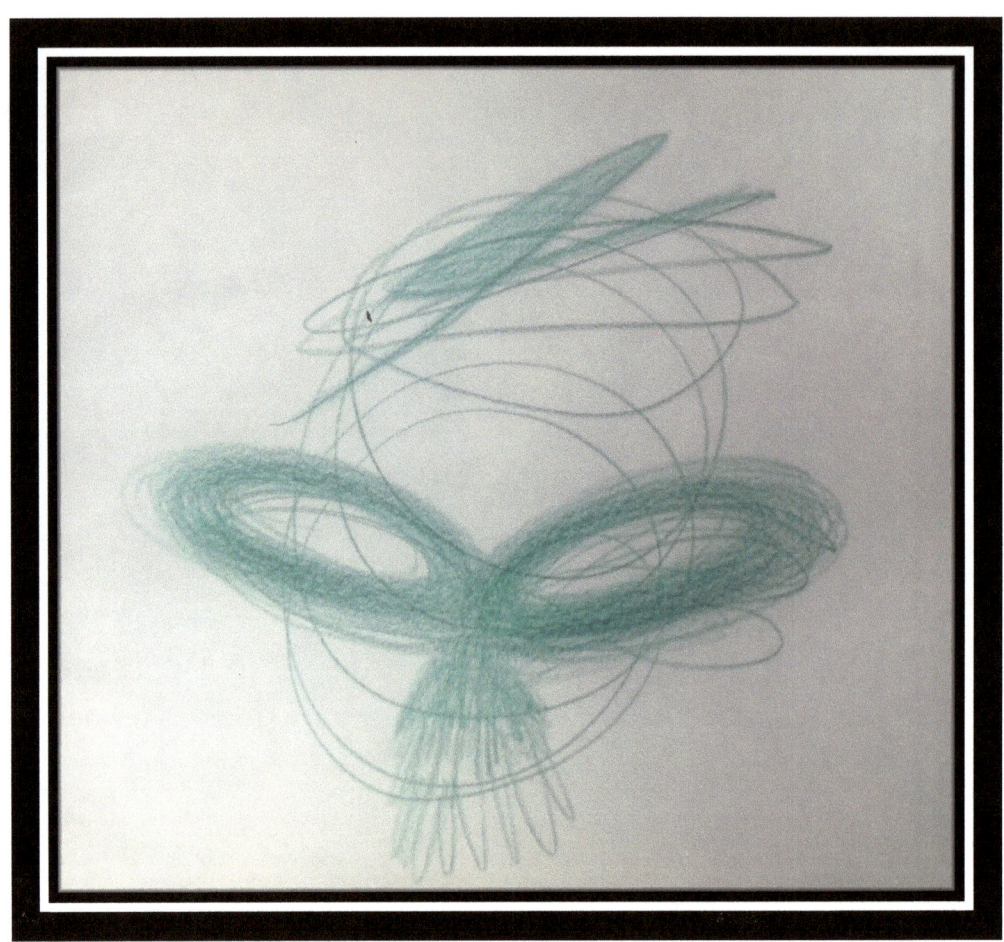

Who is the masked man?

The one who will show her the ring

Does he have 4 eyes?

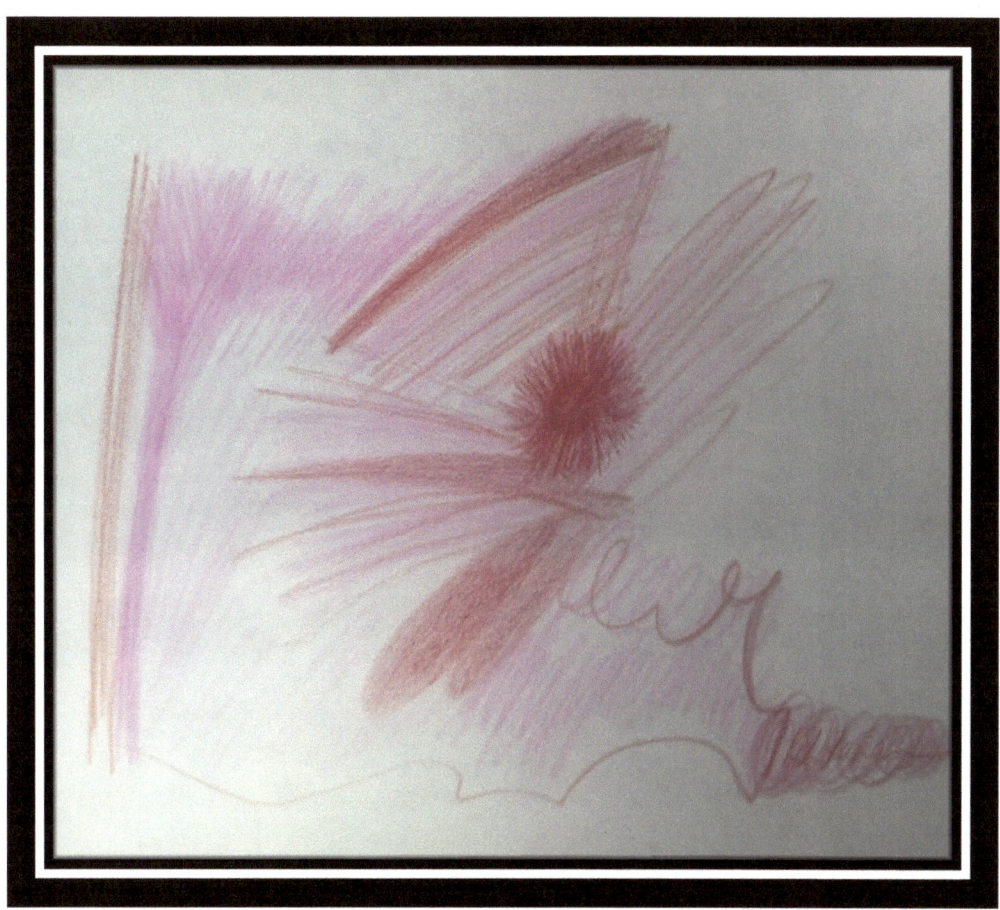

The Angel Flower-Maker

She has a thankless job

Every Spring she makes sure they grow…

You should take the time at least to stop and smell them.

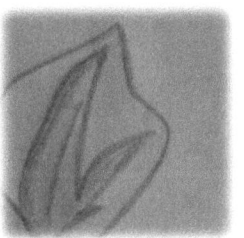

ISBN: 1514137828
ISBN-13: 978-1514137826

www.ingramcontent.com/pod-product-compliance
Lightning Source LLC
Chambersburg PA
CBHW050429180526
45159CB00005B/2465